FROM THE AUTHOR OF MONEY MY NUGGETS

YOU CAN
DO IT!

REAL ESTATE INVESTING
MADE SIMPLE

MASTER FINANCIAL COACH
KAREN FORD

CONTENTS

DEDICATION. 1
Joe Ford

ENDORSEMENTS. 3
For You Can Do It

FOREWARD. 7
You Can Do It!

INTRODUCTION. 9
YOU CAN DO IT!

CHAPTER 1. 11
 ARE YOU WILLING TO TAKE THE RISK?

CHAPTER 2. 21
HOW TO BUY PROPERTIES

CHAPTER 3. 35
RENTALS- LOVE THEM!

CHAPTER 4. 49
FLIPPING

CHAPTER 5. 61
AUCTIONS

DEDICATION

JOE FORD

To my husband who has been so very patient with me throughout this writing process and continues to believe in me - priceless! Thank you for your love for me.

KAREN FORD

ENDORSEMENTS

FOR YOU CAN DO IT

As a real estate investor myself I have to say this is a very good summary with such great examples of what you need to know before you invest. Read this book slowly, get inspired, take a lot of notes, follow the steps, go to a couple of auctions in your area. If you have more questions - follow Karen, she is the true expert!

Olga V Szakal
a Wellness Crusader and Online Marketer
who likes to simplify things
www.olgaszakal.com

As an avid reader, I can't tell you how much this book has helped me with my finances. After years of struggling with debt I started reading Karen Fords books. She is in fact a financial wizard....I recommend to anyone to buy the book and just read and possibly do what it says to do. You can't go wrong....

Michael White
Construction Worker-Dry Ridge Ky

Karen has hit the ball out of the park with this book. Whether you are an investor or new to real estate investing, this book holds the keys to making large profits with real estate investing. Truly a must read for those that think that real estate investing is difficult. Karen has removed the challenge out of the way.

Holly McKhann
www.HardHatHolly.com

Very informative. Just like anything else, there will always be risk, but real estate is probably the best way to go. You buy low, and sell high.

Mark White

Karen Ford's latest book YOU CAN DO IT is a must read for anyone who is interested in real estate. Whether you are already and active investor or a person who is interested in creating wealth through investing this book will educate you greatly! Karen's vast experience will walk you through all the things to do and not to do. This book is filled with gold that you will want to always refer back to time and time again. I love this book as there is so much wisdom on every page I truly cherish it!

Jacqui Phillips
Author, Celebrity Makeup Artist, Speaker

KAREN FORD

FOREWARD

Karen Ford has done it again! She has given us a book that informs, that instructs and that highly motivates through her own experiences on investing in real estate! This is not only an easy read but a "what did she say to do" manual that we can return to again and again to guide us thru real estate investing for prosperity!

Dr. Rebecca Polis
Coach, Teacher
Co-Founder of Faith Church Interntional

Karen Ford has written a great book for those who seek practical, tried and proven strategies for creating wealth. Karen has been successful in Money Management and Real Estate Investment and is a Certified Financial

Coach helping people get debt free and ready for retirement. As a Real Estate Investor myself, I especially like the Chapters dealing with Rentals and Flipping Houses, something Karen does very successfully. If you are just getting into a plan for creating wealth, or just need some fresh insight to add to your already working plan, You Can Do It will be a fresh resource of inspiration.

Dr. John Polis
Author, Investor, Coach, International Speaker

INTRODUCTION

YOU CAN DO IT!

There are many that desire financial freedom and one great way in achieving this goal is by investing in real estate. Many want to provide for their families, but they also want more freedom with their time, rather than having a 9-5 job at a desk and working longer or irregular hours at something less conventional.

Whether you're an avid investor or new to the real estate genre, real estate investing can be adventurous and very profitable.

In the pages of this book, you will not only discover potential risks, but rewards to investing. You will learn the keys to locating that right property as well as what to do with that property so you receive the greatest financial reward.

You will not only learn about real estate principles, but also the steps to take in giving your profits the highest potential.

CHAPTER 1

ARE YOU WILLING TO TAKE THE RISK?

Real Estate. Is it risky? It can be. Keep in mind, though, that so is about anything worth investing in.

When it comes to real estate investing, let's face it, investing equals risk. So, if you're contemplating real estate, then you need to be self aware of how much risk you're willing to take. Risk is a natural part of any investment and there's no exception in real estate.

BE SELF-AWARE!

Let's begin with the mind!

Whatever you are thinking about is what becomes reality.

It's imperative that we take notice of what we are thinking, because what we think we become.

Do you want to invest and have wealth? Then you need to begin thinking you can do it! It isn't just a mind game. It doesn't mean you are exempt from learning all that there is about investing, but be self-aware of how you think about yourself.

When we allow ourselves to be shaped, fashioned into the world's mold, we begin to think like the world, act like the world, and be like the world.

We can shape our minds. Just like a caterpillar becomes a butterfly, we can shape our minds into believing we can invest as we learn.

When our minds are in charge, then our mouths will line up with what we are thinking upon.

Begin thinking thoughts, "I can invest and I am an avid investor." Whatever you think on, you will move towards.

We should not only think with our minds, further we must speak with our mouths.

Words are powerful! I think of a large ship that is going out to sea, and what will turn that ship is the small rudder. Something so small can move such a large object.

One great thing to begin doing is to speak words that will direct you into the direction of investing.

Consider saying, "I am an avid investor and am able to learn quickly what and how to invest." Words are powerful and they are a result of what we think upon and believe. What are you believing about your finances? Because what you truly believe is what you will speak! If you want to invest, begin to think and mediate upon God's Word and speak it forth into existence!

We have discussed that we need to keep our minds and our thoughts positive. We need to ensure that our mouths, like a small rudder of a ship, will help turn our finances in the right direction. Now, we need to look at what we make. What are we doing?

We also need to DO and apply what we believe! We do what we believe. People act in line with what they believe. For example, if we believe that a stove is hot, we won't place our hand on it. If we believe that exercise is good for us to maintain our bodies, we will exercise. If we believe that investing is a good idea, then we will learn about investing and do it.

Consider a real estate investment trust, otherwise known as REIT. REIT's are a corporation which invests in real estate properties with funds from individual investors. These are similar to stocks which are sold on major exchanges and they are required by law to pay out 90% of their income as dividends.

You won't be involved with day to day dealings like a landlord, but you can enjoy the benefits of the dividends over time.

REIT'S ARE A CORPORATION WHICH INVESTS IN REAL ESTATE PROPERTIES WITH FUNDS FROM INDIVIDUAL INVESTORS.

REIT's are more than liquid assets from other real estate investments, because you can sell the shares of stock rather than selling the real estate properties themselves.

Just note that if the real estate properties drop in value, your shares of stock will most likely drop as well.

Knowing that the risks exist and determining whether or not you're going to be compensated for the risk you're willing to take is crucial to success.

There are different types of risk involved because the economy and market can't always be predicted.

Debt is one risk you need to be aware of. When people are beginning to purchase properties for rentals, flips or whatever the case may be, most start with purchasing the property with a mortgage.

Placing too much debt on a particular project can cost you in the long run. If you purchase a property for rental income and you lose some of your tenants because of college students return home, or certain jobs have closed in your area, you can lose out.

Another risk is that unexpected costs may arise because of the property condition itself. Maybe when you bought the property it all looked good, but then the furnace, which is 22 years old quits working, or the roof begins to leak.

Real estate as a whole is known for its ups and downs, as the market changes. When it's a good market, rentals are occupied. When it's a down market, you'll see lower rents being charged to get them occupied.

Geography is something else to consider as the market can vary from state to state.

Debt Maturity risk is something to ponder as well.

If your property's debt matures in a down market, then

you might not be able to get a new loan in the same amount that is your outstanding debt.

Real estate is known for its ups and downs and good markets are when you have strong occupancies and your rent amount is growing.

You can now understand how 2 real estate investments can have different risks. You as an investor must look at the risks and determine if you're going to have the opportunity to grow with the least amount of risk.

The best way to buy and invest in real estate is to pay cash for it. This ensures you own it; you won't have to tie up any money with a mortgage payment and when you sell it, you have made a profit.

Some folks won't be able to purchase properties with cash, so what will they do?

If you're not going to pay for the property outright, then I recommend that you buy it with the lowest interest mortgage you can get. This will enable you to have low monthly payments while you either renovate the property for flip or rental, or gives you time to just sell it as is until a buyer comes along.

Please note that you will need to get insurance on the

property whether you have a mortgage payment or not. If there is a mortgage payment then the bank or financial institution will require the insurance. If you pay cash for the property, please get insurance on it. You won't want to lose the property, hence your investment, due to a fire, or any catastrophic event.

NOTES:

MY IDEAS:

KAREN FORD

CHAPTER 2

HOW TO BUY PROPERTIES

There are a variety of ways to purchase real estate.

Each situation is unique so I'll cover several approaches to acquiring real estate to try to cover many possible scenarios.

MLS

The first way you could acquire property is using an MLS listing. MLS stands for "Multiple Listing Service."

This may be unfamiliar to some, but can affect the sellers goal of getting the best price reasonable possible for their home.

If a person is selling their home using MLS, their goal is for their home to have greater exposure to sell more quickly.

This is an advantage for the seller, and potential buyer.

A recent study showed that four out of five home buyers get the property they want through MLS.

When a seller lists their property on MLS, they will have most every real estate agent in the area working for them. Real Estate agents from other firms will be able to show the property to their prospective clients.

MLS STANDS FOR "MULTIPLE LISTING SERVICE."

The seller property will also appear in searches and have their property shown with more frequency.

Active marketing on MLS usually includes open houses, tours by brokers, and inclusion of the seller's property in the MLS download to other real estate internet sites.

THE REALTOR

You may consider using a realtor to purchase a property.

They might not know everything, but they do know lots of brokers and other realtors in the area you are looking.

They also know home inspectors, real estate attorneys and they will be able to direct you through the buying process.

Realtors must adhere to a code of ethics because they are licensed and belong to the National Association of Realtors. This is the largest trade group in the USA. What does this mean for you?

Under this code, they are obligated to put your interests ahead of their own. They MUST make a full disclosure about potential problems with the property.

Most savvy real estate agents can spend a few minutes in a home and search online for comparable houses and know the price range in which the home is valued at. In other words, if you are looking for a specific price range, the realtor won't waste your time by showing properties out of your budget.

A realtor will be familiar enough with local zoning to make sure you don't buy a wrong property. Let's say you want to purchase a property that is a house but you would like the bottom floor to be used for a business, a realtor would or should know the city zonings as to whether you may have a business in that location.

I have multiple properties that I acquired with the help of a realtor and one key I would like to provide you with is to make sure you and your realtor are both on the same page. What do I mean? If you are very particular and a real go-getter, then you want a realtor who also has a Type A personality so they will be like a dog with a bone. You want someone who is going to not only be assertive but aggressive in looking for properties that fit what you're looking for.

MAKE SURE YOU AND YOUR REALTOR ARE BOTH ON THE SAME PAGE

THE FSBO

Another way to potentially look for properties to purchase is through "For sale by owner sites" or FSBO.

- A great advantage of buying a FSBO is you are negotiating directly with the seller. You don't have to be concerned about a realtor telling you that your offer is too low. Realtors can be great, but at times they may tell you your offer is too low because they want to increase their commission. When buyer are able to negotiate the price without having to figure out the commission for a realtor, the seller finds this easier to give a straightforward price to the buyer.

- Rather than using an agent to help negotiate the

price, we must note that the seller is motivated to sell their house because it has a direct impact on their life. The seller may be open to giving a better price, and have a faster sale process if the buyer is pre-approved for a mortgage. Before actively looking for a property you might consider going to your bank or mortgage lender so they can take your application information and get you pre-approved for a mortgage loan. Many times, this will have a positive impact upon you and the seller. You'll know exactly how much you're pre-approved for and the letter that the mortgage lender gives you will be a pre-approval letter, which can motivate the seller to sell to you rather than others who don't have this letter. By giving them a copy of the letter, they know you can get the money.

"FOR SALE BY OWNER SITES" OR FSBO

- When you work with a realtor, you are waiting for them to provide your questions to the seller and waiting for the agent to get back with you with the sellers answers. If you buy a FSBO property, then you will be talking directly to the seller and this saves TIME! You will also avoid any potential misunderstandings.

25

- Please note that when you are looking for a FSBO, you are going to need to do your own research. What are the other homes (comps) in that neighborhood valued at? What were those other homes sold for? You may need to make a trip to the assessors office located in that county to see the value of the home when it was bought. It doesn't matter what you think as a prospective buyer, comparable sales for the areas determine the market value of that home. For example, if the seller tells you they have updated the bathrooms and completed many renovations and their 3 bedroom 2 bathroom home is worth $300,000 but the other 3 bedroom 2 bathroom homes in the same neighborhood are selling for $210,000 then that's quite a difference and most likely their home will not appraise for the $300,000 price tag they have on it.

- Once the price is agreed upon between the seller and the buyer, now comes the paperwork. With a FSBO you don't have the advantage of a realtor to look out for your best interest. Without your own representation, you'll have to review the sales contract yourself or just hire a real estate attorney.

THE FORECLOSURES AVENUE!

Foreclosures are another great way to acquire homes and land. Bank owned properties are a great way to get your hands on a great deal, because the banks want to get these properties sold to get them off their books.

When a bank takes a property back, after forclosing on the owner, the title to the property will be clear, so the buyer won't take any liens or have to pay back taxes from the previous owner. The house will be vacant so you'll only need to set up the time to view it according to the bank's schedule. Some foreclosures will be listed on MLS with a real estate agency representing the bank, so in most cases the bank will pay the real estate commission.

> FORECLOSURES ARE ANOTHER GREAT WAY TO ACQUIRE HOMES AND LAND.

Some disadvantages of buying a foreclosure are the bank will NOT do any repairs and you'll purchasing it "as is."

Some banks won't provide disclosures as to the property history or condition, so you'll need to do your due diligence when walking through the property and inspecting it well.

Now, let's look at foreclosure auctions, as these are slightly different.

One great aspect of a foreclosure auction is the property will be sold for the outstanding mortgage balance owed. This could potentially be a much lower price than the property value.

A downside to this is most auctions in this way require

> FORECLOSURE AUCTION IS THE PROPERTY WILL BE SOLD FOR THE OUTSTANDING MORTGAGE BALANCE OWED.

a cash on the day of the auction. Also, you won't be able to do any inspections and you'll need to do your own research for title or back taxes or liens.

Let's say a property is getting ready to go into foreclosure but it hasn't yet. The seller may be advertising "for sale by owner" or some banks may provide information about these types of properties.

Let's face it, if the seller has missed so many payments their property is going to be foreclosed on, they will be motivated to sell fast and a great opportunity for the buyer to get a below market price.

The buyer will be able to get inspections and regular mortgage financing.

The seller still has to provide the buyer with the property's condition and any problems with the property.

As the buyer, you might not be able to negotiate the price below the outstanding balance of the mortgage. So if the owner/seller still owes $120,000 on a $150,000 home, you're not going to be able to buy it for less than what the seller owes.

I have bought properties because they were foreclosed on and the listing price was good but I wanted a better deal. I told my realtor what I wanted to pay and she looked at me like I was nuts. I told her to write it up anyway. The price was $20,000 less than what they were asking. The forclosing agency kept coming back with the response, "We cannot sell it for that price but will sell it to you for this price." The price they countered with was the asking price they listed it for. I kept coming back with $1 increments increase. In other words, if my offer was $38,000 I would re-counter with $38,001 and then the next day, after receiving it, their counter would be their listing price. This went on for 2 weeks. My offer came up to $38,015 by the time it was done. I am sure they got tired of having to respond to my counter offers and finally let me purchase the property for that price.

AUCTIONS

A lot of auctions for properties are the typical public auctions at said property.

A great advantage is that the buyer will be able to purchase the home for a deep discounted price. Some auctions don't have a reserve price.

This brings me to my next point. There are typically two types of auctions: Absolute and Secured Auctions. The secured auctions means the seller wants a certain amount of money for the purchase. The auctioneers are aware that the seller must get a certain amount. The Absolute auction is where the property will be sold to the highest bidder- no matter what

> SECURED AUCTIONS MEANS THE SELLER WANTS A CERTAIN AMOUNT OF MONEY FOR THE PURCHASE.

that price is. For instance if a property is valued at $100,000 and the auction for it is absolute then if the highest bidder that day is at $50,000 then that's it! The buyer got a great deal just because it was absolute.

Typically, closing will happen quickly with an action, usually within 30-45 days.

A few cons to buying properties at auction are many auctions are cash deals, and the buyer must have those funds available and ready. This can also work in the buyers benefit, because some potential buyers won't have the cash to purchase the property so this decreases the number of bidders.

Another con to consider is that auction homes are sold "as is." The buyer will be able to inspect the property on the day of the auction, but that isn't always the case. If you buy a home through an auctions, you should make sure you have money for potential repairs or any renovating you plan upon.

I have bought several properties at auction and one great example is there was a property being sold for absolute. It was a snowy week and I knew there wouldn't be as many people showing up for the auction. This property was a two story brick colonial home with 4 bedrooms and 2 bathrooms. The auction terms were read and the bidding began. It came down to the wire between another couple and myself. The look on their face revealed that they were reaching the bid limit. I bid one more time and got the property. The moral of this story is, when you're bidding, pay close attention the expressions on the face of those you're bidding against. You might get the property with one more bid.

> ABSOLUTE AUCTION IS WHERE THE PROPERTY WILL BE SOLD TO THE HIGHEST BIDDER- NO MATTER WHAT THAT PRICE IS.

NOTES:

MY IDEAS:

KAREN FORD

CHAPTER 3

RENTALS- LOVE THEM!

Let's talk about rental income. This isn't for the faint of heart. You must do your due diligence. Why would you want to invest in rental properties?

***Tax Benefits** – Investing in real estate allows for many tax benefits.

1. Interest- You can deduct interest from mortgage payments on loans. Certainly, I recommend that you pay cash for the property, rather than having a mortgage payment to deal with on a rental property. If you choose to buy the rental property using a mortgage, keep in mind that banks and mortgage holders will ask if this will be your residence. When

the loan is made for a rental, most mortgage holders will require 20% for a down payment plus closing costs.

2. Depreciation- The owner can deduct the cost of the property over several years. It benefits your taxes by way of depreciation if the property is providing you an income.

3. Repairs- Any repairs are deductible in the year in which they are done. This enables you to deduct the cost of those repairs. Keep good records on each property. For example, if you replace a hot water tank, be sure you have the receipt and mark on the receipt which property it was for. The receipt should have the date and location of the purchase. You should then mark on the receipt the address for which property.

4. Insurance- You're able to deduct insurance premiums that have to do with your rental property. This includes liability, flood insurance, fire and theft. Please note, that the insurance for the property is for the dwelling alone, not for the tenant's property. When meeting with tenants, let them know that the insurance on the property does NOT include coverage of their belongings and recommend

they get renter's insurance. This is generally not expensive and will protect them.

*Appreciation - Rental properties usually increase with inflation. So if inflation occurs, your rental income can increase. Real estate appreciation occurs when home values rise because of businesses, popularity of the area, or neighborhood growth. Think about homeowners that bought their home 20 years ago. They bought it for a good price, and now their home may be valued with $150,000 equity. Now, looking at rental property. Let's say you purchase a rental and rent it out for 20 years. This would be a great source of income and most likely has also increased in value.

*Retirement Income - Rental properties can be a great preparation for retirement income. Income from rental properties is considered passive income, but it doesn't mean that it's effortless. Purchasing rental property will not only create a great income for retirement, but also allows you to sell it at a higher price in the event you want to sell one of your rental properties in the future.

We have a couple in our city who are preparing for retirement and they have several rental properties which brings them in over $12,000 rental income each and every month. This is a great way to have another income stream.

Another couple has over $800,000 in rental properties which yields them a whopping $18,000 per month- each and every month.

How do you determine the property will be a rental? This question needs to be answered long before you purchase it. Check the neighborhood or area in which the property is located. Are there other rentals in this location? If so, what is the rental income of those properties? Do they stay rented or are there college students that move out frequently? Is there trash out for days or unmanicured lawns? When contemplating the purchase, check for neighborhoods where the properties are cared for. These are things that will help you determine if this is in a location that you want to rent.

Something else to consider is single tenant vs multi tenant units.

Single tenants are great because by definition its 100% leased.

If you have a multi unit building, then it's rare it would be 100% vacant.

How much rent can you charge for the house you're buying?

This is a great question and needs answered before you sign on the dotted line for purchasing the property.

The amount of rent you can charge your prospective tenants should be a percentage of the home's market value. This is generally between 0.7% and 1.1% of the value. So if the home is valued at $100,000 then the rent could be between $700- $1100 per month.

If the house is valued below $100,000 then the rent should be closer to the 1.1% value.

You may want to consider what other property owners are charging for rent in that particular location. Charging $300 more per month than other rentals in the area can cause you to have an empty rental for a period of time. Remember, the goal is for you to make money on the rental income, and if it's not rented, you're losing out.

> REMEMBER, THE GOAL IS FOR YOU TO MAKE MONEY ON THE RENTAL INCOME, AND IF IT'S NOT RENTED, YOU'RE LOSING OUT.

You might not be able to charge whatever rent you want, because some states have a limit on what you can charge. For example, New York, California, Maryland all have rent control laws. If you plan on investing in these states, then do your homework and familiarize yourself with the laws in your state.

Now that you've located the property and made your purchase, who will you rent to?

Don't get in a hurry to rent your place. Of course you want to rent it as soon as possible so you can start making money, but don't be in such a hurry that you rent to the first person that shows interest.

Place a "For Rent" sign in the window of the property. Advertise the rental on social media, in newspaper, and by word of mouth.

You'll start getting phone calls to see the property.

It's necessary to check out each potential renter because the old saying is "You can't judge a book by it's cover." They might sound good and look good, but will they pay their rent on time? Will they keep the home clean? After interviewing the clients, discreetly drive by the home in which they live now. Chances are if they are not taking care of their present property, they won't take care of yours.

I highly recommend that once you have selected the tenant that you have them provide you a copy of their driver's license and sign a lease. The lease can be a year, 6 months, or even month to month. Stipulate in the lease what they are responsible for and what the landlord is responsible for. There should also be outlined a late fee if the rent isn't paid on time.

This protects you and they know this information upfront when renting from you.

Keep in a file for each tenant, the lease, rental application, copy of their driver's license, copies of their pay stubs, and any other pertinent information. Any time the tenant contacts you, document the conversation and place the date and time on it and place it in their file. In the event you ever have to go to court, you will have records that will be valuable. We don't want to rely on memory alone. I had to evict some tenants because of non-payment of rent and I was so thankful I had every conversation documented as well as dates the rent was promised and not paid.

Explain that the lease is a legally binding contract. The tenant is bound for the full amount of the lease. If the rent is $1200 per month then the full amount in one year is $14,400. They will be responsible for this amount even if they decide to move before the lease is up.

Put a clause in your lease that states if they break the lease, you can charge a lease breakage fee of one month's rent and that they would surrender their security deposit. Make sure that you check in your state and local laws to be sure you can do this. This will cause the tenant to think twice before breaking that lease with you.

If for some reason that tenant breaks the lease in no fault of their own, such as a job transfer, you can waive that fee, especially if you can get it rented quickly.

I had a tenant who I rented to, she and her father. They paid the rent on time each month and kept the place clean and tidy. They weren't noisy and I never had any complaints from neighbors about them.

She called me one day and said that because of her father's ailing health they would have to move out of state so he could get the proper care from a particular physician. I certainly understood that and explained that she was breaking the lease, but if she would have it cleaned when she moved out, we would do a walk-thru together before they left and no additional charges would incur. She and her father left with a good rental report and I was able to rent it again after they moved.

PROTECT YOURSELF AND YOUR PROPERTY.

In the event you have to evict, because of non-payment or damage to the property, you will need to check with the magistrate court in your area to steps to do so. Many states require that the person be served a certified letter stating

YOU CAN DO IT!

the eviction. I can't say this enough. Protect yourself and your property.

I have an 8 page lease which the tenant is required to read before signing. Have I had to evict someone? YES! I didn't want to have to do this, but they left me no choice. Don't let your heart get in the way of not evicting. They broke the lease in some way, otherwise you wouldn't be evicting them.

I have had great tenants. Paid on time, took care of the place, and I've had tenants that were late with rent and had to pay the late fees.

One couple who rented, had rented from us for 8 years. They kept the home clean and tended to the mowing of grass and paid their rent on time. I could have rented to them for another 8 years, but they ended up buying their own home.

I'm not saying that all of your tenants will be stellar, nor am I saying that you'll end up with tenants that you have to evict. What I'm saying is do your research and ensure you protect yourself and your property.

Are you going to be the person who collects the rent each month or receives the phone calls for potential repairs?

If so, then know that you'll need to keep good records and expect phone calls any time of the day.

I recommend that you have a property manager. A property manager is a person who advertises the rental to be rented, interview prospective clients, keep records, will collect the rent on your behalf each month and receive the phone calls from the tenants for any repairs. If repairs are needed, the property manager will make the necessary phone calls to get the repairs done quickly.

The property manager typically receives a payment of 10% of the rent.

So if you have a rental unit which is $1000 per month then the property manager will receive $100 per month, pay you the remaining rental income and they will receive the phone calls.

When you interview for a property manager, the same thing applies. Have an agreement that you both sign. This agreement should stipulate the conditions of the agreement and what each of you is responsible for. Some real estate agencies may have realtors who work for them that also manage properties.

A property manager can be a valuable asset, especially if you have more than one rental property.

A woman had 17 rental properties she was managing and would clear around $20,000 per month for just that.

NOTES:

MY IDEAS:

KAREN FORD

CHAPTER 4

FLIPPING

Are you ready to flip your lid or flip a house? Flipping a house can be fun but at the same time very challenging, and it can also be a great money maker. In this chapter I'm going to touch on all of those things.

Some great benefits to flipping a house are :

1. One of the main reasons folks want to flip a house is because they want to make money. This is a great reason for sure, and if it's done right, a flip can provide large profits in a short period of time. But this isn't the only reason to flip.

2. There's so much experience that you can gain from

flipping a house. When you purchase the materials for the flip, you'll gain negotiating skills and the ability to manage your time in a greater way, hold people accountable and learn and practice delegating tasks.

3. By renovating a property, you'll gain a greater understanding of the costs of materials and perhaps learn how to repair some plumbing and electric.

Budgeting is another key aspect in which you will be "baptized in fire" if you're flipping for the first time. If you're not an avid budgeter, then you'll learn rather quickly not only the costs associated with flipping, but how to manage your finances better and you'll end up making the most profit on your flip.

So when you've decided you're going to search for a property to flip, how will you know if it's going to be financially lucrative for you? Determine your budget for purchasing a house first. Then you will know how much you're able to spend on the property. Check auctions, for-sale-by-owner opportunities, realtors, and websites for properties in your price range as well as the geographic locations in which you're considering. You might consider making notes and drive by the potential homes and take pictures, so that memory doesn't have to be depended on.

YOU CAN DO IT!

Once you locate prospective properties, check the comps in the area. What are 'comps'? Comps are "comparable sales" in real estate terms that will compare the house you're presently looking at to others in the same area, which are similar in square footage, condition and features. You will want to look at comps because this will help you decide what price you should offer and whether the home is appropriately priced.

COMPS ARE "COMPARABLE SALES"

If the home you're looking at is a 3 bedroom, 2 bathroom home, then check other 3 bedroom, 2 bathroom homes in that same area and see how much they sold for. This can quickly determine if you're going to flip this particular house. For example, if the house you're looking at has a selling price of $80,000 and other 3 bedroom 2 bathroom homes in that area sell for that price or less, you might consider not flipping it. However if that house is for sale at $80,000 and other homes in the area sell for $150,000 then it may be a consideration to flip, barring no structural damage or mold which can be very expensive to rectify. Once you decide which house you're going to flip, then make your offer. My rule of thumb is to offer less than the asking price. If you offer the asking price, then that's it. They will most likely accept that offer and now you have no where else to go on the price. If you offer lower, there's room to negotiate between you and the seller. You want to get the best possible price you can so you can make the necessary changes to it and flip it for considerably more.

I purchased a home which already had a furnace, central air and hot water tank, and were all only 1 year old. We bought the house for much less than the asking price, and we began to work. We ended up putting in a new kitchen, 2 new bathrooms, new windows, new carpet and flooring with fresh paint on the interior. A lovely young couple with 2 small children purchased this as their first home. This was very rewarding as they got a great newly renovated home and we made a significant profit.

TIMEFRAME

How long should it take to flip a house? This question certainly has validity and needs answered BEFORE you close on the purchase of any house you purchase with plans to flip. When you walk thru the house, you should have ideas on what changes need to be made. If this is your first flip, be sure to check the prices of products you want to purchase and check with your contractor or handyman what his labor will entail. For the most part, you will know what renovations you plan on doing, the cost of those supplies and the cost of the labor.

When I flip a house, my ultimate goal is to have it completed in 30 days. Now, this would be simple cosmetics: paint, carpet and staging. I have flipped houses which took longer, but knowing what you plan on renovating and replacing are keys to determine the amount of time it will take. In other words don't buy a house to flip without having an end date in mind. If you do this, it may take you 6 months, 9 months or even a year. The longer it takes you to flip it, the market may change. So make a plan!

If you plan on replacing a kitchen and 2 bathrooms, the flip will take longer, but be sure you discuss the end date with your contractor or handyman who will be doing the work. Be sure when you set up the agreement with the person overseeing the project, that you get the agreement in writing. Many times, your job isn't the only job they are working on. They juggle many homes and projects, so if you have a contract stating the date it's to be done, this applies some pressure to them to be done in a timely manner. A written contract is something that will hold up in court, if you ever have to use it. Verbal agreements are just that, verbal.

When I make plans for the flip, I let my contractor/handyman know upfront that I will buy all the materials required and I want to know his cost for labor. This keep my thumb on the pulse for the cost of the project as a whole.

Because I've done flips, I already know what most materials cost and I can then negotiate on the cost of labor. Don't automatically say yes to the price the contractor gives you. If you can, always get estimates from a few contractors and get those estimates in writing. If you have more than one, the power of negotiation is in your hands.

COSTS - When flipping, determine your budget for the renovations you want to make. Go to your local home improvement store and make notes of costs of particular items: bathroom fixtures, appliances, drywall, paint, carpet and flooring. This will give you an idea or rough estimate on the prices of such items, so you can make plans for your flip. There are times when you take possession of the home and begin tearing out walls to renovate, when you may discover plumbing that needs replaced or a furnace or central air unit has stopped working, which will cost you above the predetermined amount you planned on spending.

> IT'S BETTER TO PLAN FOR THE UNEXPECTED THAN NOT PLAN AND HAVE THE UNEXPECTED HAPPEN ANYWAY.

When you evaluate and make your plans for the costs of flipping a house, I recommend you add 20% on top of that cost. Why? Because unexpected things will happen.

It's better to plan for the unexpected than not plan and have the unexpected happen anyway.

So if the cost of painting, renovating 2 bathrooms and replacing carpet is going to be $50,000, then put in your budget 20% more, which will be $60,000.

You can cut costs on materials in a variety of ways. Many times home improvement stores will provide a discount to veterans, as well as to contractors and certain other groups. Watch for special sales too. Some will offer deals when you replace windows or a discount for carpet and many times we have had them give us deals on carpet with free installation. Another way to cut costs are in the purchasing of paint. Many paint stores you call carry "oops paint" or "mistint paint." This is paint which was mixed for another customer and they either didn't like the tint once mixed or it wasn't mixed properly. Some paint stores will sell this mistint paint for $1 per gallon. When I was preparing to close on a home I was going to flip, I went to the paint store and got 20 gallons of interior, neutral color paint for $20. This brings me to the point of interiors colors for your flip. Most people want to visualize their furnishings in this home, so a bright blue or red wall may not be the way to go. When you choose paint colors, lean more towards neutral colors. It will be much easier for the potential buyer to see themselves living there when the walls are cream, light grey or beige.

Once you have all the renovations completed, now it's time to stage the home. Depending on the market you're in, you may get by without staging the home. Placing furnishings and wall hangings in the home actually gives the potential buyer an idea of how their own furniture will fit. This can work to your advantage, as it's challenging for the potential homeowner to see what their furnishings will look like in various rooms.

You don't always need a professional stager. I have gone to a rent-to-own store and staged the home with their furnishings for less cost. I explain that the house is a flip and it's staged for showings. This gives them relief as the furnishings will be returned to them undamaged. They will deliver the furnishings and set them up. I generally only stage the home in this way for 30 days. The rent-to-own store charges per month, and once the furniture is set up in the home, pictures can be taken and house showings begin. If the house isn't under contract by the time the furnishings are removed, the pictures will still provide enough information for the potential buyers.

MARKETING

Now it's time to market it. You have options here. You could have an open house and show it yourself using fliers with pictures and price of the home, or you can utilize a real estate agent. One thing we learned in a previous chapter is that an agent will have more time to show the property than you will. When hiring an agent, be sure they are on the same page as you. Assertiveness is key when showing and selling the property. Remember when you list the property, the agent will get commissions, so work that in your plan if you plan on using a realtor.

ASSERTIVENESS IS KEY WHEN SHOWING AND SELLING THE PROPERTY

Some flippers actually like to have an independent appraiser walk thru the house and appraise the property BEFORE they list the property. This can also work to your advantage, as they will give you a unbiased evaluation. Keep in mind though, that depending on the market and how busy appraisers are, you might end up waiting for a period of time. If you plan on getting an appraiser to the property before you list it, then call 2-3 weeks BEFORE you plan on listing it. Make sure when the appointment is set, that the appraiser comes to a COMPLETED property. Don't waste their time or your time by having them attempt to appraise a property that's not completed. This can shoot you in the foot so to speak.

We bought a home in a local city and I had my handyman walk thru with me and he made notes on what I wanted done. He also made some suggestions, which actually made the home more marketable and cost effective. We had the carpet removed on the second floor because there were oak hardwood floors underneath, and on the first floor, we had new carpet installed. We had both bathrooms renovated and the kitchen updated. We then had the entire interior painted and all the windows replaced. We sold the house within 60 days of putting it on the market and made a $35,000 profit.

NOTES:

MY IDEAS:

CHAPTER 5

AUCTIONS

Many states have a State Auditor's Office. State auditors are executive officers who serve as controllers and auditors of state funds. In West Virginia, they also handle properties that have been sold to the state for non-payment of property taxes. People actually do lose their properties because of not paying taxes. Property owners could be delinquent on their taxes because the owner doesn't have the money or perhaps they passed away and the relatives didn't know or just don't pay.

Within the state auditor's office, there is a county collection division and their role is to return tax-delinquent lands to private ownership. This is accomplished through redemption of property and offering the parcels at public auction. You will want to check the status of properties in your own particular state, but in WV once taxes on various properties have not been paid, the state auditor's office will acquire the property as a tax lien and give the owners 18

STATE AUDITORS ARE EXECUTIVE OFFICERS WHO SERVE AS CONTROLLERS AND AUDITORS OF STATE FUNDS.

months to redeem the property. If the property hasn't been redeemed, then after 18 months they certify the property to the Deputy Land Commissioner for public auction. This is where you have the opportunity to

purchase properties at a drastically reduced rate. Call your state auditor's office for dates of the upcoming auctions and ensure you get to the auction early. They may be required to post the property addresses in the newspaper as well as on their website, so you'll have time before the auction to search them out.

Please check the rules and procedures for purchasing properties in your state. Other states may offer properties through bidding online or may hold their auctions more frequently than once per year.

Before the auction begins, the state auditor's office will place the list of properties that will be sold at auction online. They will have the person's name, county, tax year it was sold to the state auditor and some real estate terminology which would provide a general vicinity of the location of the property. It will be up to you to do your due diligence and check online or do some research at the county assessor's office. By looking up the person's name and general location of the property, you will be able to locate the address and even drive by the property to see the general condition. You'll also be able to discern if the property is inhabited with people or not.

As a general rule, check the roof, windows, and foundation. If the roof and windows are intact, then it's safe to say that no animals have taken over the inside. If the roof has issues or there are broken windows, you might end up choosing not to bid on the property.

We purchased a property and the roof was intact, and it didn't appear that there were any foundation issues and there weren't any broken windows. About two weeks before we got the deed to the property; however, some vandalism was done and there were broken windows. By the time we received the deed and entered the property, feral cats had taken over. Needless to say, there was quite a mess to clean up. We hired some folks to remove all carpet, clean it up and secure the properties with padlocks and cover the windows. We ended up selling the property to someone who was going to renovate and live there.

In WV, properties will begin with the bidding of $10. Now, this isn't to say that the bid will stop there, but I have purchased properties for $10. The bidding may go up, depending on the location, if there is a building on the property etc. I purchased some properties with mineral rights at the auction. This can also be lucrative, because when the gas companies drill, royalty checks are given to the owner of those mineral rights.

Once all the bidding is complete, you pay for them in the tax office. In WV, the state auditor office will then send a letter of notification within 30 days to the buyers at the auction stating they approved the sale and also send some necessary paperwork. This paperwork will need filled out by an attorney. If you choose to do the title deed search, please note that in the event the property gets redeemed, you won't be eligible to be reimbursed for the purchase of the property if you don't utilize an attorney. The attorney will do his due diligence and check if there are any heirs to the property. In WV, any relatives would need notified of the property being sold at auction and give them the opportunity to redeem the property. Most of the time, the properties remain unredeemed. In WV, they have until the day that the deed is recorded to redeem the property, so note that you won't own it until that time the deed is recorded.

Then the attorney will send the state auditor's office the paperwork and the purchaser waits. If the property is redeemed, the money spent at auction is refunded to you the buyer. If the property isn't redeemed, the auditor office will then send you a fee to be paid for recording of the deed. This may seem like a long process, but once you do this, it can be very lucrative. Once you have the deed in hand, the property is yours.

I once bought a property sight unseen (I don't recommend this) but I knew the general area. I paid $10 for the property, paid $300 to the attorney and paid $50 for the recorded deed. I ended up selling the property for $1400. This property was interesting, because although I knew the location, I hadn't set foot on the property. It was a trailer on a lot, and there was a padlock on the door and a large sign which read "Uninhabitable- Meth house." So, how was I to sell this gem to someone? I marketed it just as it was. Advertisements said "Trailer on lot- trailer was a meth house and is uninhabitable. Trailer will need removed from property." I had someone that desired the lot and was willing to remove the trailer. I had the attorney make a note on the deed that the seller "me" notified the buyer "them" that the trailer was uninhabitable and would need removed from the property. All bases were covered and we closed!

I also bought a house at auction for $700, paid $300 for

the attorney, and $50 for the deed recording, and sold it for $5000. The house was in disarray, but was worth getting the $5000 for it. Another property which I purchased through an auction, paying just $1500 for it and just had the contents removed and the grass mowed. We sold it for $35,000. Once you receive the signed deed, you own the property. Any items left inside the property now belong to you. You can choose to sell those items or just have someone remove them if you don't want to take the time to sell the contents.

We had looked at a property, which we knew was going to be sold at the state auditor's auction and on the property was a vehicle. About two weeks before the auction, that vehicle had been removed. Had that vehicle still been on that property when we received the deed, we would have owned that house and the vehicle! Remember, that when you receive the deed to a property, the contents and whatever items are on the property now belong to you! This can be a positive or negative aspect. If you purchase a property and there are items that are not salvageable, then you'll need to get rid of them.

We had purchased a house and there was a large piece of land next to the house, that included a large amount of junk on it; which included, piles of lumber, old bathtubs, porch beams, sinks, lots of tires. The city office had contacted us and told us that once we received the deed, we would need to remove those items since they were an "eye sore." It would have taken at least 15 large dumpsters to remove all that material. Long story short, we re-investigated the property lines of our house and the land with all the junk on it, was NOT ours. We contacted the city back and told them they we would not be responsible for this. Now, had we not done our investigating, they may have kept that insight to themselves and would have gladly allowed us to remove those items. The owner of that lot had to remove those items.

There may be properties which you buy for a less amount of money, but that doesn't mean you can't sell it. There always seems to be a buyer for the property that we purchase.

Now, some of the properties may sell for much more. There was a large piece of property with several acres and in a prime location next to a shopping mall. The property was assessed and valued at $650,000 but then man who won the bid only paid $25,000 for it.

Purchasing properties at a state auditor auction is lucrative but requires patience. In WV, they hold this auction once a year in each county. So, you can actually do your research and perhaps go to various county auctions. I do recommend that you get the list of properties before the auction, as they will have a list, and take a day or two to see where the properties are located and what kind of condition they are in, before you decide to bid on them.

CONCLUSION

After reading this book, you should have gained core principles to making real estate investing a great success.

You now hold the strategic keys to unlocking an investing adventure. If this will be your first or fortieth time in purchasing property, my hope is that you gain the financial freedom you desire. Real Estate investing can be challenging, but it is so enjoyable and a key to building wealth.

Believe in yourself - you can do it!

NOTES:

MY IDEAS:

OTHER BOOKS BY KAREN FORD

MONEY NUGGEST:
Quotes that will change how you think about money and
inspire you to build wealth.
Beg, Borrow, or Budget ... Control Your Money and
Change Your Life!
In this uplifting book, Karen Ford motivates you to think
differently about your money and encourages you to start
building wealth today!

**31 DAYS TO A GREATER
UNDERSTANDING OF MONEY:**
Biblical Principles to Help You Get Out of Debt & Enjoy
the Life God Has For You
Does God care if you are prosperous?
Do you struggle with your finances?
How can you gain control of your money and live free
from the stress of issues surrounding money?

MONEY MATTERS:
Motivation, Methods, and Manners for Increase.
Does God want me to have money?
Why does He want me to have money?
How do I get the money God wants me to have?
Learn the answers to these questions and more in Money
Matters!

**AVAILABLE AT
KARENFORD.ORG & AMAZON.COM**

KAREN FORD

Made in the USA
Middletown, DE
18 June 2021